ENVIRONMENTAL DISASTERS

Love Canal

Pollution Crisis

by Nichol Bryan

WORLD ALMANAC® LIBRARY

Please visit our web site at: www.worldalmanaclibrary.com
For a free color catalog describing World Almanac® Library's list of high-quality books and multimedia programs, call 1-800-848-2928 (USA) or 1-800-387-3178 (Canada). World Almanac® Library's fax: (414) 332-3567.

Library of Congress Cataloging-in-Publication Data available upon request from publisher. Fax (414) 336-0157 for the attention of the Publishing Records Department.

ISBN 0-8368-5508-6 (lib. bdg.)
ISBN 0-8368-5515-9 (softcover)

First published in 2004 by
World Almanac® Library
330 West Olive Street, Suite 100
Milwaukee, WI 53212 USA

Copyright © 2004 by World Almanac® Library.

Produced by Lownik Communication Services
Cover design and page production: Heidi Bittner-Zastrow
Picture researcher: Jean Lownik
World Almanac® Library art direction: Tammy Gruenewald
World Almanac® Library series editor: Carol Ryback

Photo Credits: Cover, 15, 39, © Galen Rowell/CORBIS; 4, Heidi Bittner-Zastrow; 5, 6, 7, 12, 14, 22(b), 23, 27, 30, 31, 34, 36, 37, © Bettmann/CORBIS; 8, 22(t), 35, © Mug Shots/CORBIS; 9, © J A Giordano/CORBIS SABA; 10, © Kevin Fleming/CORBIS; 11, © Derek Croucher/CORBIS; 13, © Paul A. Souders/CORBIS; 16(b), © Charles E. Rotkins/CORBIS; 16(t), Courtesy of the U.S. Bureau of the Census; 18, 26, 29, © Wally McNamee/CORBIS; 19, © LISA BUNIN/GREENPEACE; 21, © Michael Philippot/CORBIS SYGMA; 24, © Tim Wright/CORBIS; 28, © Digital Art/CORBIS; 33(b), © Greenpeace; 33(t), © Michael Heron/CORBIS; 38, © Palmer/Kane, Inc./CORBIS; 41, © Joseph Sohm; ChromoSohm Inc./CORBIS

Printed in the United States of America

1 2 3 4 5 6 7 8 9 07 06 05 04 03

Cover: The 93rd Street School was one of many buildings abandoned after toxic waste bubbled to the surface in the Love Canal area of the City of Niagara Falls, New York.

Contents

Love Canal

NEW YORK

 # Introduction

"Every Mother Is **Scared To Death**"

Love Canal began as one of the twentieth century's brightest dreams. It turned into one of the century's darkest industrial nightmares.

As the 1900s began, the Love Canal neighborhood — located in the City of Niagara Falls in New York State — was a place where people expected the future to be born. It would serve as a showplace of the new era, filled with clean homes and spotless, efficient factories. Everything would run on that new miracle power source: electricity. Love Canal promised to show the world

A Red Cross nurse takes a blood sample at the 99th Street Elementary School in August of 1978. New York state officials wanted to determine the extent and effects of the chemical contamination.

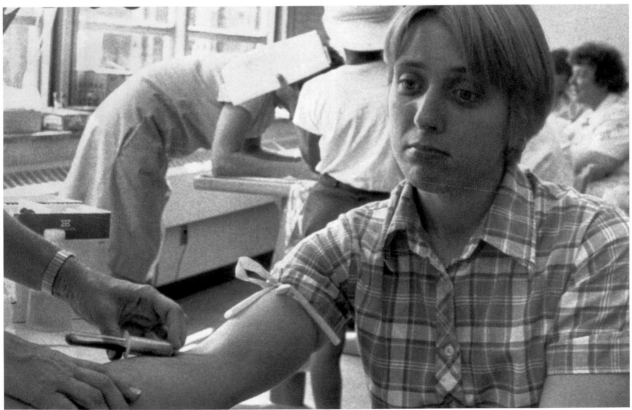

how technology and industry would soon make people's lives better, happier, and longer.

Eight decades later, Love Canal was an abandoned ghost town, its decaying homes and overgrown lawns a silent testimony of fear. Residents fled the 15-acre (6-hectare) neighborhood after many people began to have health problems and eventually learned that Love Canal had been built over tons of toxic waste. Heavy rains brought pools of slimy, foul-smelling chemicals bubbling to the surface of lawns and schoolyards. Children began to come down with strange diseases. Scientists discovered the toxic sludge contained chemicals like benzene and dioxin — substances that can cause cancer and birth defects.

In 1978, after the toxic mess at Love Canal gained the attention of the entire world, President Jimmy Carter declared the neighborhood a federal disaster area. Up until that point, federal disasters were declared to help people recover from damage caused by the forces of nature, such as floods, earthquakes, drought, and wildfire. Love Canal was the first federal disaster created by humans.

Love Canal became a national scandal, one that would change the United State's history. It drew the attention of millions of people to the environmental movement, which gained widespread momentum in the late 1960s. Before Love Canal, environmentalism was largely the concern of a handful of political

The once family-filled Niagara Falls suburb of Love Canal was abandoned and run-down by 1980 — two years after the evacuation.

Dioxin? Or Something Worse?

"Every mother in the Love Canal is scared to death, wondering who will be the next one with leukemia symptoms. Will it be her child, her neighbor's child, or even herself? Every family watches and wonders what the spring thaw is washing to the surface, scared of what their children might be walking in, playing in, or falling in. Is it dioxin? Or something worse?"

— Love Canal residents
Mr. and Mrs. Joseph Dunmire,
in a letter to New York
Governor Hugh Carey,
April 27, 1980

water pollution and industrial waste seemed much closer to home.

The Love Canal crisis raised important new issues in the nation's environmental debate. Who is responsible for cleaning up the toxic waste left behind by factories and businesses? What happens when the polluter is a corporation that no longer exists? Should a company be able to cover a toxic-waste dump with dirt and just walk away?

How much of a role should city and state governments play in pollution disasters — especially when cleanup and restoration may cost millions or even billions of dollars? When should

activists and some concerned citizens worried about environmental quality. The fact that industrial pollution had turned a quiet, middle-class community such as Love Canal into a wasteland served as a wake-up call for average voters. People just like them had lost their homes and were watching their children die. Suddenly, issues like

No softball today: Eleven-year-old Joel Guagliano sits outside a fence in his Love Canal neighborhood where chemicals seeped up through the ground in 1978.

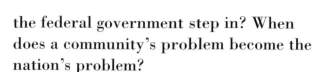

the federal government step in? When does a community's problem become the nation's problem?

One of the biggest changes that grew out of the scandal of Love Canal was a bigger, more powerful Environmental Protection Agency (EPA). The federal agency was still fairly new when the crisis loomed. Now the Agency found itself handling an emergency that not only required the evacuation and relocation of hundreds of families, but also the settlement of their medical claims. Occidental Petroleum had purchased Hooker Chemical — the company that caused the pollution — years earlier. The EPA needed new powers in order to handle such a crisis — and to somehow prevent future disasters.

Congress responded by passing tough new laws giving the EPA broad power to sue companies not directly responsible for pollution

Toxic-waste workers discuss cleanup operations at a different site ten years after the crisis at Love Canal.

Do you live near a Superfund site?
Thanks to the Environmental Protection Agency (EPA), it is easy to discover how close you live to an active Superfund site or to a Superfund site that has been cleaned up. Visit the EPA's web site to find the city, name, street address, and EPA site number for Superfund hazardous waste locations in every U.S. state.
http://map3.epa.gov/enviromapper/index.html

Forest Glen Park Community was a mobile home site built on a toxic waste dump near Love Canal.

in order to pay for the cleanup. The new laws, officially called the Comprehensive Environmental Response, Compensation, and Liability Act (CERCLA), stated that a corporation that bought another corporation was responsible for any pollution caused in the past by the company about to be purchased. Also, any contractors that transported toxic waste from site to site had to pay for problems caused by that waste. Furthermore, companies that created any type of pollution had to pay into Superfund — the name by which CERCLA became popularly known. If a site needed cleaning and the government couldn't sue the responsible

polluter, some of the cleanup money came from Superfund.

Superfund seemed like an ideal response to problems like Love Canal. The EPA soon discovered other toxic waste sites and designated them as "Superfund sites." It turned out that thousands of polluted sites existed all over the United States. Today, one out of every four Americans lives within

4 miles (6.5 kilometers) of an identified Superfund site.

Americans' attitudes towards the environment have changed many times since Love Canal. The United States continues to wrestle with environmental issues. Voters have always cared about clean air and safe drinking water. They also care about their jobs and taking care of their families. Certain politicians claim that too much environmental regulation hurts businesses — which causes job loss and puts people out of work. Many politicians say regulations are either/or choices that hurt people financially in order to help the environment. But the situation is often far from being that simple.

Environmentalists point out that although it seems costly to change to different manufacturing techniques that create less pollution, in the long run, society pays a heavier cost when pollution isn't controlled and people get sick because of it.

Thanks to Superfund, Love Canal was eventually cleaned up. At the end of the twentieth century, after two decades of work and after spending $250 million, the EPA ruled that most of the land around Love Canal was safe. Slowly, people began to move

Not Unique

"Isn't the Love Canal problem unique, you wonder? Sadly, no. Its only uniqueness lies in its being the first. Beyond the Love Canal lie an estimated fifty thousand other chemical dump sites in the United States. All those other thousands may be spewing unimaginable quantities of poison into our water, land, and air. The bitter harvest of that which has been planted is now being reaped — ecological disaster and human tragedy."

— From a report by the Ecumenical Task Force of the Niagara Frontier

back into the Love Canal neighborhood, buying the once-abandoned homes that had been refurbished and remodeled. Economics drove the resettlement — property in Love Canal was relatively inexpensive compared to other areas.

But a portion of the neighborhood — the part closest to the old canal — remains fenced and is off-limits to residents. The ground in that area is still so full of toxicants that people may never be able to live there again.

 Chapter 1

Love's
Model City

When most people look at Niagara Falls, they see a thundering tribute to nature's power and majesty. But when William T. Love looked at the Falls in 1892, he saw the future.

Love was a flamboyant entrepreneur who liked to think big. Like many people in his time, he was excited by the coming twentieth century and its promise of technological wonders. Love wanted to be part of that future. The City of Niagara Falls, still an untamed border town in western New York State, was just the place to make his mark.

Love had a vision of a great canal that would circle around to the south

Niagara Falls borders western New York and southeastern Ontario, Canada. At one time, the lip of Horseshoe Falls — also known as the Canadian Falls — was breaking off and moving up the Niagrara River at a rate of more than 3 feet (1 meter) per year. Large water-diversion projects built in the 1950s and 1960s slowed the rate of erosion. Now it takes about thirty years for the Falls to recede that same distance.

A new park was created for the 1893 World's Columbian Exposition in Chicago. The Exposition was also known as "White City" because of the many temporary white-plaster palaces built just for the event. One building was recreated in masonry after the fair as The Field Museum, which serves as Chicago's natural history museum today. The Electrical Building is pictured above.

of the mighty Niagara Falls. Love's canal would have locks that allowed ships coming up the Niagara River to bypass the Falls and enter into Lake Erie. From there, ships could move through the Great Lakes to reach booming industrial towns like Cleveland, Detroit, and Chicago.

But the canal would do more than move ships: It would provide a rushing stream of water to turn massive turbines for generating electricity. The idea of harnessing electricity for light, heat, and power was brand-new in the 1890s. The World's Columbia Exposition in Chicago in 1893 awed visitors with its enormous Electricity Building showing inventions by Thomas Edison and Nikola Tesla. People were especially dazzled by the Exposition's great White City, which blazed at night thanks to those new electric lights.

For Love, the electricity generated

Love's New Model City
If you get there before I do
Tell 'em I'm a comin' too
To see the things so wondrous trueAt Love's new Model City

— An advertising jingle promoting Love Canal (circa 1893)

by his canal would make this futuristic vision a reality for average people. He dreamed of building "the most perfect city in existence," which would become home to more than a million people. Those people would have jobs in factories powered by electricity — not by coal with its black smoke and soot. Cheap power would make Love's model city clean, luxurious, and perfect.

To build this dream, Love needed to locate his community close to a power source. That's because early electric projects used direct current, or DC power. Electricity is caused by electrons moving through a wire. In DC power, the electrons move directly through the wire in one direction only, so it's called direct current. Direct current was easy to generate, but the voltage, or intensity, of the current varied according to the location on the DC line. Engineers thought that power plants needed to be built every block or two in order to meet the electrical needs of homes and factories.

Love's dream for the area wasn't exactly new. Canal building to divert

Power lines are a common sight today. Engineers once believed that electricity could not travel over long distances. They thought that many, many power plants needed to be built close to where people lived and worked.

Nikola Tesla was a Croatian-born naturalized American physicist, electrical engineer, and inventor. He discovered that magnetic fields rotated, which led to the use of alternating currents in electrical machinery. This technology allowed electrical current to travel long distances over wires.

water to power flour mills and machinery had begun at Niagara Falls before the Civil War. A water-driven electric generator was installed in 1881. But Love had a more complete vision — easy ship transportation, cheap power, and a model community. He got financial backers and began to dig the Love Canal in 1893.

It did not take long for the future to catch up with William T. Love — and to pass him by. In the mid-1890s, Tesla proved that generating a new form of electricity, called alternating current, or AC, was more economical for home and industrial use than DC. In AC power, electrons constantly reverse direction at regular intervals as they travel through the wires. This alternating motion prevents them from losing energy as they move longer distances. Alternating-current power could be sent long distances over wires, which meant that fewer

generators farther away were necessary for power. There was no longer any need to build a model city right next to a canal.

Economic downturns that plagued the nation around the turn of the century dried up Love's funding. Investors also lost faith in his glorious vision of a model city. Love dug less than 1 mile (1.6 km) of his canal before abandoning the project. The completed portion — 3,000 feet (914 m) long and about 100 feet (30 m) wide — was paved with clay and for years was used as a swimming hole by local residents.

By 1920, the land Love had purchased for his model city had been bought by a local power company. The power company offered it as a dumping site for the City of Niagara Falls and nearby factories. In 1942, one company in particular became a frequent user of the dump site — Hooker Chemical and Plastics Corporation. Hooker made

agricultural chemicals, fertilizers, plastics, and various chemicals used in manufacturing. The company used the canal to dump chemicals left over from its operations. From 1942 until 1953, Hooker dumped more than 21,000 tons (19,000 tonnes) of chemical wastes into Love Canal.

The Chemical Revolution

Hooker was just one of thousands of new industries that boomed during and after World War II. New discoveries in chemistry led to the development of products that were better and cheaper. Plastics seemed to hold special promise. Developed during the war as a replacement for scarce metals, plastics could be used to make nearly anything from toys and dinnerware, to radios and furniture. Agricultural chemicals, such as fertilizers and pesticides, also appeared to offer a future of plentiful

food and the elimination of hunger.

All these products, and many more, relied on the use of a bewildering array of new industrial chemicals. The U.S. production of industrial chemicals, such as sulfuric acid, increased as much as six hundred percent from 1940 to 1970.

While science made great strides in creating new chemicals in the postwar years, the impact of these chemicals on human health was less well understood. Plant operators knew the more obvious effects of direct contact with these substances — vomiting, blindness,

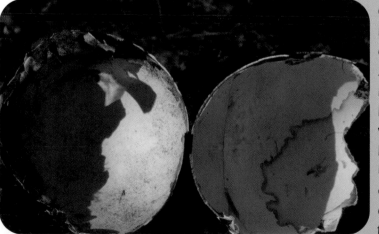

Exposure to DDT caused many birds to lay eggs with thinner than normal shells that often broke before hatching — killing the baby bird inside.

DDT: the first big chemical scare
Dichlorodiphenyltrichloroethane (DDT) was the first toxic chemical to come to the nation's attention. In 1962, scientist Rachel Carson warned that this commonly used pesticide could find its way from farms and orchards into water supplies and the food chain. As people and animals consumed small amounts of DDT, it built up in their bodies, causing disease and death. Carson's book, *Silent Spring*, is named after an imagined future in which most birds and animals had been wiped out by pesticides. Carson's book became a best-seller in the United States and raised a storm of controversy about the use of chemicals in agriculture. When the Environmental Protection Agency was formed, one of the first chemicals it banned entirely was DDT.

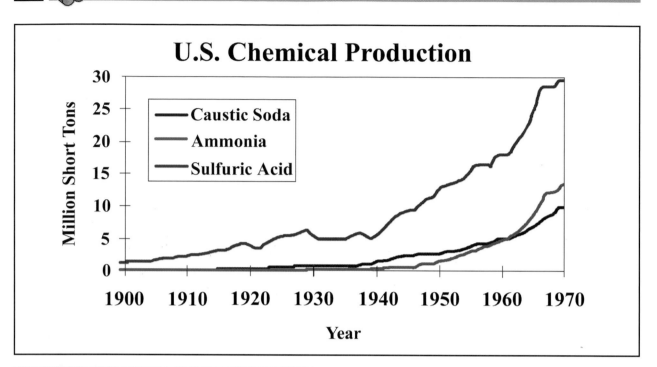

U.S. Chemical Production

Legend:
- Caustic Soda
- Ammonia
- Sulfuric Acid

Y-axis: Million Short Tons (0, 5, 10, 15, 20, 25, 30)

X-axis: Year (1900, 1910, 1920, 1930, 1940, 1950, 1960, 1970)

A researcher checks greenhouse plants for nutrient levels at an early growth stage. Hooker Chemical produced a large range of agricultural chemicals and fertilizers.

and chemical burns — and took steps to protect workers from them. It wasn't until the 1960s that scientists began to understand that exposure to even small amounts of some of these chemicals could cause cancer, birth defects, and other serious problems. By then, hundreds of tons of chemicals from a variety of sources all over the United States had been released into the environment. Some leaked out of dumps where chemical waste products were stored. Others were applied directly onto the land and water in the form of agricultural chemicals.

By the late 1960s, more and more citizens of the United States became interested in protecting the quality of their air, land, and water. Activists protested against all sorts of toxic releases. In 1970, under pressure from the environmentalists, President

Richard M. Nixon urged Congress to create the Environmental Protection Agency. Its mission was to regulate pollution and set guidelines for the use and storage of toxic chemicals.

But all this was still far in the future when Hooker Chemical was dumping toxic waste at Love Canal. The company did take some precautions to contain the chemicals. It lined Love Canal with concrete to help prevent the chemicals from leaking out into the surrounding groundwater. When the canal was completely filled with waste, Hooker built a ceramic and clay cap over it, and then covered the cap with soil. The field created over the canal was used by local children for soccer and baseball games.

Meanwhile, the city planners of Niagara Falls had their eye on the undeveloped land around Love Canal. Their community was expanding rapidly in the post-World War II baby boom. People were looking for new homes. The city considered the Love Canal area an ideal place for a new housing development. Hooker Chemical hesitated to let go of the land, which it knew concealed a toxic graveyard. But the city threatened to seize the land anyway, so the company sold it to the Niagara Falls School District in 1953 for $1.

The papers transferring the property included a warning that the property contained a chemical landfill and released Hooker from any liability for problems at the site. The warning went unheeded, however, and soon single-family homes were springing up around Love Canal.

An Unheeded Warning

New homeowners and builders were never told what lay beneath the soil at Love Canal. They dug basements and sewers, unaware that they sometimes punched holes in the concrete walls and ceramic cap of the canal. To meet the children's needs in the growing community, the city built a brand-new elementary school, the 99th Street School. It was located directly on top of the old canal.

An Early Warning

"Upon my arrival at the Hooker dump, the wind was blowing from a westerly direction and the area was permeated by odor of chemicals and fumes emitting from a pile of chemical waste at the dump. . . . This unknown substance was an irritant to breathe and obnoxious to smell and it is my opinion that this material could be a detriment to the health and well-being of residents in this area."

— From a note by
Niagara Falls Fire Chief Edwin Forster,
dated November 2, 1964

Activist Lois Gibbs

The Love Canal crisis transformed stay-at-home mother Lois Gibbs into an environmental crusader. In 1978, the 27-year-old Gibbs learned that her five-year-old school sat on top of a toxic waste dump. Worried about how the toxic chemicals affected the children, Gibbs circulated a petition throughout the Love Canal neighborhood to close the school. She also organized the Love Canal Homeowners Association, which fought to get the state and federal governments to pay for the relocation of people living near the canal. Her efforts to get Congress to pass a law providing for the clean up of toxic-waste sites earned her the nickname "Mother of the Superfund."

Gibbs' outspoken criticism of Hooker Chemical and the government won her national attention. She testified before Congress and spoke at many environmental rallies. Gibbs became a regular fixture on television, appearing on shows such as *60 Minutes*, *20/20*, and the *Oprah Winfrey Show*. Many environmental groups asked for Gibbs' help, so in 1981 she created the national organization now known as the Center for Health, Environment and Justice (CHEJ) and serves as its executive director. CHEJ helps people eliminate dioxin sources in their areas. A television movie, *Lois Gibbs: The Love Canal Story*, was made about her life in 1990.

In 2001, CHEJ helped warn about other schools built on toxic-waste sites. Gibbs again testified before Congress in 2003 about how adults must protect the nation's children from toxic emissions that contaminate the air, water, and soil. She received many honors for her work, including the Goldman Environmental Prize and the Heinz Award in the Environment, named in memory of U.S. Senator John Heinz III, who helped pass the Clean Air Act Amendment of 1990.

At first glance, the Love Canal neighborhood was like any of the hundreds of similar housing developments that sprouted up all over America in the 1950s. But the proud homeowners clustered around Love Canal gradually noticed that something wasn't right. The air smelled strange. Sometimes, after a heavy rain, flooded basements became stinking pools. Strangely colored puddles formed in people's lawns. The city reacted to the resident's many complaints by covering the oozing puddles with clay.

Residents in Love Canal began noticing other things. Many children were being born with birth defects. Adults were getting sick, too, with diseases like cancer. Women were losing their babies before birth. Although tragedies such as these happened to people everywhere, every day, they seemed to happen more frequently at Love Canal. Was it all just coincidence?

The complaints continued, so in

Former Love Canal resident Barbara Quimby and daughters, Courtney (left) and Brandy (right) stand in front of their Grand Island, New York, home. Very possibly because of her exposure to the chemicals that seeped from Love Canal, one of Mrs. Quimby's children was born with birth defects. Mrs. Quimby has since had an operation so that she would never have children again.

1976 the city hired a consulting firm called the Calspan Corporation of Buffalo, New York, to look into the problems at Love Canal. The firm reported toxic chemicals in the air and in the basements of homes at the south end of the canal. It also discovered rusting 50-gallon (189-liter) drums just below the surface of the soil over the canal. To make matters worse, the water in the storm sewers contained high levels of polychlorinated biphenyls (PCBs) — cancer-causing substances found in some industrial chemicals.

Calspan recommended that the city take steps to control the toxic leaks in the neighborhood. It urged the city to build a new clay cap over the canal and install a drainage system that would lead contaminated rainwater away from the housing areas. But the city planners took no action and they failed to inform the residents of Love Canal what the Calspan report had discovered.

Also, the EPA produced an internal report on the situation at Love Canal in 1977. Although it, too, discovered unhealthy and hazardous conditions, no warning was published or issued to the general public.

And so the people most in danger of being harmed by the toxic chemicals lurking in Love Canal knew nothing about them.

"A Faint, Choking Smell"

"I visited the canal area at that time. Corroding waste-disposal drums could be seen breaking up through the grounds of backyards. Trees and gardens were turning black and dying. One entire swimming pool had popped up from its foundation, afloat now on a small sea of chemicals. Puddles of noxious substances were pointed out to me by the residents. Some of these puddles were in their yards, some were in their basements, others yet were on the school grounds. Everywhere the air had a faint, choking smell. Children returned from play with burns on their hands and faces."

— Eckardt C. "Chris" Beck, former EPA Assistant Administrator for Water and Waste Management, appointed in 1979

Chapter 2

A New Kind of Disaster

In the mid-1970s, the secrets of Love Canal began to spill out — literally.

In 1975 and 1976, western New York got a large amount of rain and heavy snowfalls throughout the winter. All this extra water flowed into the buried canal through the holes unwitting builders had punched in its side. The canal filled up and overflowed, causing toxic streams to flow through the neighborhood. Rain also washed away parts of the soil covering the canal, exposing countless drums of poison.

The neighborhood's problems, once just annoying, now turned into a nightmare. Noxious odors were everywhere. Basements filled up with an oily ooze, and the pumps people put in to get rid of the mess were eaten away by corrosion. Illnesses were

Corroded, leaking drums holding toxic waste were found at Love Canal, New York.

"Unknown Chemicals in Dubious Containers"
"Unhealthy and hazardous conditions exist at the landfill and in some of the homes adjoining the site. Surface drainage is poor; surface water goes through the landfill rather than over and away from it. Unknown chemicals in containers of dubious condition permeate the landfill in unknown numbers and locations. . . . To correct the problem will be expensive and will draw on the resources of several levels of government. It is estimated a long range complete cleanup program will cost in excess of a million dollars."
— From a 1977 internal EPA report on conditions at Love Canal

reaching epidemic proportions. Children came home from the 99th Street School with chemical burns on their arms and legs after splashing in the toxic puddles. Homeowners began to panic. What was going on?

Then, in April 1978, reporter Michael Brown helped clear up the mystery. He wrote a series of articles in the *Niagara Gazette*, revealing the area's toxic past. Brown discovered that many of the chemical plants located along the Niagara River had left behind toxic dumps and landfills. Many were leaking, endangering the health of nearby residents. The leaks also threatened the quality of water in the surrounding lakes and rivers. One

Actress Jane Fonda appeared at the Capitol in Albany, New York, in 1979. Fonda was promoting the idea that the State of New York should buy more homes in the Love Canal area and move residents to other housing.

Tim Moriarty, 66, sits on the porch of the Love Canal home he has lived in for thirty-five years. His sign refers to the availability of toxic chemicals in the ground underneath the porch. Moriarty was forced to move because of the chemicals.

of the biggest of the forgotten toxic dumps, Brown said, was Love Canal.

People in the neighborhood were stunned. Most had no idea they had been living over a chemical landfill. Suddenly, things started to make sense — the smells, the mess, the mysterious illnesses. Outraged, residents demanded that the City of Niagara Falls and the State of New York pay attention to their long-standing complaints.

But New York State had already begun to move. The Department of Health had collected air and soil samples and conducted health studies. On April 25, 1978, the New York State Commissioner of Health, Dr. Robert P. Whalen, proclaimed Love Canal a public health hazard. Whalen ordered the Niagara County Health Department to clean up exposed chemicals at the Love Canal site and to install a fence around the entire landfill site. Suddenly, Love Canal was big news — not just in New York — but throughout the United States. The Department of Health and the EPA launched new investigations. Frightened, angry residents met with state, city, and county officials to determine what to do about the emergency. National television news stories focused on Love Canal as an example of a new toxic threat the country faced.

For Love Canal residents, the revelations were both a blessing and a curse. At last government officials were taking them seriously and they were starting to get some answers — but the answers were shocking. They and their children had been exposed to chemicals

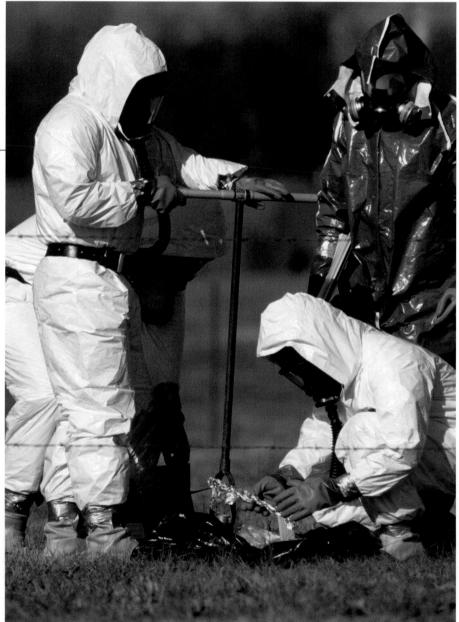

A "haz-mat" (hazardous materials) team cleans a dioxin spill in Virginia. Dioxin is an extremely hazardous chemical. Workers study how to best clean each type of chemical or hazardous-materials problem. Team members must wear safety gear, including full-body protective suits, face masks, special respirators, gloves, and boots. Duct tape seals their sleeves to their gloves and their pant legs to their boots.

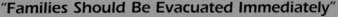
"Families Should Be Evacuated Immediately"

"Toxic chemicals are presently migrating through the soil along the paths of old streambeds that once crisscrossed the neighborhood. Families whose homes border these old streambeds show an increase in several health problems including miscarriages, birth defects, nervous breakdowns, asthma and diseases of the urinary system. These studies have led me to conclude that a minimum of 140 additional families should be evacuated immediately and evacuation may need to be extended to as many as five hundred more families."

— From 1979 Congressional testimony by Dr. Beverly Paigen, EPA cancer research scientist

that could make them sick for the rest of their lives. Naturally, most residents wanted to leave. But how could they escape from Love Canal? Who would buy homes near one of the nation's most notorious toxic dump sites?

At the end of that summer, the crisis deepened. In August, Dr. Whalen declared a health emergency at Love Canal. He recommended the immediate evacuation of children and pregnant women from the two rows of houses closest to the canal site. Whalen also ordered the closure of the 99th Street School because it was built right over the canal.

The State of New York stepped in to help the panicked residents of Love Canal. New York Governor Hugh Carey announced that the state would purchase all the homes immediately surrounding the dump site. But it was clear that more steps were needed.

Toxicants were flowing from the site

to all parts of the neighborhood and into local waterways. To buy out the residents, help them with their medical bills, and clean up the mess would cost the State of New York a staggering amount of money.

Then on August 7, 1978, President Jimmy Carter stepped in. He declared the dump site and those first two rings of houses around it a federal emergency area. For the first time, a federal emergency was declared for a situation that was caused by humans and not an act of nature. The declaration meant that the costs of Love Canal fell under the authority of the Federal Emergency Management Agency (FEMA), the federal agency that provides aid to victims of disasters.

Federal money would permanently relocate 239 families living closest to the canal. But the declaration ignored people living in the rest of the ten-block area of the Love Canal community.

Two Big Offenders: Benzene and Dioxin

Investigators found hundreds of different toxic chemicals at Love Canal. Two that caused the biggest health worries were benzene and dioxin.

Benzene is used to make plastics, detergents, pesticides, and other chemicals. Hooker Chemical used a lot of it in its manufacturing process. Benzene causes cancer. People exposed to benzene regularly for as little as five years have developed fatal cases of leukemia, a cancer of the blood. The federal government determined that breathing air with more than one part per million of benzene can be harmful. Benzene can also be absorbed through the skin. Children who played in benzene-contaminated puddles probably absorbed significant amounts of benzene into their systems.

Dioxin is actually a name for hundreds of related chemicals, many of them highly toxic. Dioxin is formed as a by-product of chemical manufacturing and other industrial processes. Exposure to dioxin can cause skin lesions and liver problems. Dioxin is also suspected of causing miscarriages, birth defects, and developmental problems in children. Relatively small amounts of dioxin are produced in industrial processes, but it is so toxic that an extremely tiny amount can cause health effects in humans.

Many of the toxins at Love Canal were carcinogens and mutagens. Carcinogens are cancer-causing agents; mutagens are substances that cause cell

President Carter's Declaration

"I have determined that the adverse impact of chemical wastes lying exposed on the surface and associated chemical vapors emanating from the Love Canal Chemical Waste Landfill in the City of Niagara Falls, New York, is of sufficient severity and magnitude to warrant a declaration of an emergency.

". . . I have authorized Federal relief and such actions as are necessary to save the lives and protect property, public health and safety or to avert or lessen the threat of disaster."

— President Jimmy Carter, August 7, 1978

President Jimmy Carter ordered the paid evacuation of families living at Love Canal. He started the process for the federal cleanup program that became Superfund.

Pastor Kermit Robertson greets members of his church in 1980. Two days after Robertson arrived in Love Canal in 1978, the news about the problems broke out. A fence surrounds boarded-up homes near the church.

"A Terrible Fear"

"What has happened to the people of the Love Canal district is very nearly as destructive as a tornado. The homes still stand, to be sure, the water and electricity still run. But there may be sickness and death in the homes, and there is already a terrible fear. . . .

"What has happened to the people of the Love Canal is a disaster. Not the kind of disaster anybody is used to, but a disaster all the same."

— From an August 3, 1978, editorial in the *Niagara Gazette*

damage. Carcinogens and mutagens harm people by affecting their DNA. DNA is the material in every cell that tells it how to divide and reproduce. It functions as a "code" for building the body. This DNA code is made up of a string of proteins. The order of these proteins must be just right for the new cells to be healthy and do their job normally.

Certain substances can change the order of the proteins in a cell's DNA. This change is called a mutation. Sometimes mutated cells just die. Other times they start to divide very fast, out of control. This wild cell division is what causes cancer.

Chemically caused mutations can also affect the sperm cells in men and the egg cells in women. These mutations

A DNA molecule resembles a twisted ladder that holds the code to life. The rungs of this ladder are formed when two strings — or strands — of chemical compounds called bases bond together. The order of these bonds on the DNA ladder form a code that determines what type of protein gets made. Each section of a DNA molecule that holds the code for a specific protein is called a gene. One gene may involve hundreds of links. Genes direct what traits, such as eye color, body size, or flower color, appear in that person, animal, or plant — and what will get passed along to the offspring of that organism.

change the DNA code that tells the cells how to make a healthy baby. When this happens, or when a mother who is expecting a baby is exposed to mutagens, the child can die before it is born. Or, it can be born with serious physical problems or birth defects.

Health data gathered by the EPA showed just how devastating these chemicals had been to the people living in Love Canal. Data revealed that miscarriage rates increased more than three hundred percent for those moving into the neighborhood. A staggering fifty-six percent of children born to Love Canal residents from 1974 to 1978 — which included the period when heavy rains caused the most flooding in the area — were born with birth defects. Some of these were easily correctable problems, such as webbed fingers or extra toes. Other problems caused by the exposure to the various chemicals were more tragic, including deafness, mental retardation, and heart defects.

Adults, too, were suffering. Those living in the wettest areas of Love Canal had a seven-times greater risk of mental illness and emotional problems. Reports of depression and suicide were also on the increase. But no one knew how much of this was caused by chemical exposure, and how much was caused by the stress of living in what was coming to be known as one of the world's most poisonous neighborhoods.

Chapter 3

Life In a
Pressure Cooker

After years of neglect at Love Canal, things were starting to happen fast. Not all of it was good news for the residents there.

State and federal agencies began intensive studies in the neighborhood, and they made grim discoveries. In April 1979, investigators reported that the levels of dioxin at Love Canal were one hundred times higher than previously measured. Traces of toxins were turning up farther and farther away from the actual dump site. Contaminants were discovered six blocks away at the 93rd Street School. In months, that school was closed, too.

Love Canal became a symbol for environmentalists. Messages that appeared on the posters, buttons, and T-shirts caused an emotional response in the people affected by chemicals buried in Love Canal.

Signs warning residents to keep out were posted all over the area when cleanup efforts started in Love Canal.

Students from both schools were assigned to other schools around the city.

Also in April 1979, more federal money began to arrive. The EPA approved $4 million for cleanup work at Love Canal. The City of Niagara Falls received an additional $1 million in federal disaster assistance to help pay for its cleanup efforts.

The cleanup effort at the canal was truly massive. Contractors dug up and hauled away about 1.5 million cubic feet (40,000 cubic meters) of soil from the area. A huge drainage area was dug around the site, allowing

Increased Birth Problems

"Our findings are consistent with the possibility that a slight to moderate excess of spontaneous abortions and/or low birth weights might have occurred on 99th Street and historic water sections of the Love Canal area."

— Nicholas Vianna, M.D., from a study on pregnancies in the Love Canal area contaminated runoff to flow into specially designed containment tanks. The toxic water was then trucked to a special treatment facility where the poisons were removed.

The 99th Street School was torn down to make way for a new clay cap over the old canal. Engineers hoped that the heavy clay would prevent more water from seeping into the canal, causing it to overflow once again. Many contaminated homes around the canal were destroyed. In all, the cleanup work took twenty-one years to finish, and cost $250 million.

FEMA provided many kinds of assistance for Love Canal residents.

The agency paid for six months of rent-free temporary housing for evacuees. The agency helped pay to board up the abandoned homes and paid for security guards to patrol the empty streets. FEMA funds went to pay for day-care and day-camp programs for affected children as well as counseling programs for adults.

Meanwhile, the press descended on Love Canal. The area had become the

Love Canal refugees Robert and Jo-Ann Kott and family had to abandon their home. They were relocated to a motel and lived there until they found another home.

"I Want to Die."

"I want to tell you about my son. As I said before, he's ten, he's a bright boy, he has a 91 average in school. As a baby he never required much sleep, he was put on a sedative at about age seven months to about eighteen months, he developed rashes, frequent bouts of diarrhea and respiratory problems. His first year at 99th Street School, Kindergarten, he was admitted to the hospital, very ill. The diagnosis — acute gastroenteritis — cause unknown.

After that, more respiratory infections, tonsillitis. At age six, his tonsils and adenoids were removed, but the respiratory infections did not improve — he developed asthma. In 1977, we were told to consult an allergist. He was tested and found to have many allergies. He has been on a desensitizing program now for a year and a half, with no improvement.

By this time we the people were well aware of Love Canal, as were our children. My son went into a depression, withdrawing from the school. . . . He begged to leave. I promised we would leave soon!

One night last winter I got up to go to the bathroom. I looked in on his bed, his bed was empty. I looked all over. It was 2:00 A.M. I heard a cry from under the couch. My son was under there with his knees drawn up to his chin, crying. I asked him to come out, and what was wrong. His reply, 'I want to die, I don't want to live here anymore — I know you will be sick again and I'll be sick again.' My husband and my son and I cried together that night."

— Love Canal resident Anne Hillis, testifying before Congress

nation's most serious environmental crisis, and journalists from as far away as what is now Russia flocked to the area. They took pictures of the fenced-off canal, and of the workers in hazardous material suits removing barrels of toxic waste. Some of the residents of the area were interviewed more than one hundred times by newspaper and television reporters.

Across the United States, Americans were angered by the reports coming out of Love Canal. It was bad enough that honest, hard-working citizens were losing everything they had because they were never told about the dangers of the land they were building on. But even worse was the revelation that Love Canal was not an isolated case. It turned out that industries in communities all over the country had been quietly burying toxic waste — often on sites that were later abandoned or turned into housing developments. Some environmentalists were estimating that as many as fifty thousand similar

The Environmental Protection Agency (EPA) gained strength following the discovery of the toxic wastes at Love Canal. The EPA establishes federal limits on air pollution, sets water quality standards, determines sources of water pollution, monitors radiation levels, and monitors the disposal, handling, and control of hazardous wastes and chemicals.

waste sites had been created in the United States. Few of them were being monitored for leaks.

The Love Canal crisis gave the environmental movement a huge weapon in its campaign for tougher pollution controls. They called on the federal government to be more aggressive in enforcing pollution laws and in going after companies that tried to abandon toxic wastes. The Carter

"A Reminder to be Ever Watchful"

"The profound and devastating effects of the Love Canal tragedy, in terms of human health and suffering and environmental damage, cannot and probably will never be fully measured.

"The lessons we are learning from this modern-day disaster should serve as a warning for governments at all levels and for private industry to take steps to avoid a repetition of these tragic events. They must also serve as a reminder to be ever-watchful for the tell-tale signs of potential disasters and to look beyond our daily endeavors and plan for the well-being of future generations."

— From a report by the New York State Department of Health

Tony Manganero (right) and neighbor Steven Delles move furniture from a home on Black Creek, near Love Canal. Manganero's parents had lived in this home for twenty-five years, but moved to Pennsylvania after the discovery of the toxic chemicals.

Administration promised to take action.

All this attention made the people of Love Canal feel like they were living in a pressure cooker. They were being interviewed, studied, and pitied — but few were getting any real help. Most residents wanted to get out, but their homes had no value. The cleanup work in the neighborhood was releasing more noxious vapors into the air. Feeling trapped, many families began to fall apart. The divorce rate and drug and alcohol abuse increased; many residents sought treatment for mental illness.

Eventually, more and more residents got help leaving Love Canal. In September 1979, the state government moved two hundred people into nearby hotels after they complained of the vapors from the cleanup work. Eight months later, President Carter declared another federal emergency, freeing up funds to allow seven hundred families to leave the area.

One of the most frightening reports came in 1980. The EPA announced that eleven of thirty-six Love Canal residents tested had genetic damage. The study was later criticized because it had not been properly reviewed before publication and contained statistical errors. But it heightened the fear that the health of Love Canal residents were at risk. By the end of 1980, Love Canal began to look like a ghost town.

Chapter 4

"Shovels First, Lawyers Later"

As the cleanup work at Love Canal went on, the struggle to find the guilty parties started in the state and federal courts. One of the most obvious targets was Hooker Chemical and Plastics Corporation. After all, Hooker had dumped most of the toxicants in Love Canal in the first place.

But officials at Hooker claimed the company bore no responsibility at all. They pointed to their repeated warnings at the time of the $1 sale to the Niagara Falls Board of Education. They also pointed to provisions in the deed that released Hooker from any future damages. Besides, Hooker was no

Toxic waste cleanup is dangerous, expensive, and time-consuming. Congress established Superfund in 1980 so that hazardous waste sites can be identified and cleanup can begin before lawsuits are settled.

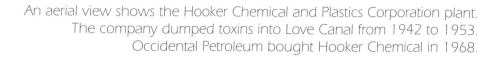

An aerial view shows the Hooker Chemical and Plastics Corporation plant. The company dumped toxins into Love Canal from 1942 to 1953. Occidental Petroleum bought Hooker Chemical in 1968.

longer an independent company. It had been purchased in 1968 by Occidental Petroleum, a huge oil conglomerate which renamed it Oxy Chemical. Any lawsuits would be against Occidental, not Hooker.

But the residents of Love Canal disagreed. More than 640 of them filed lawsuits against Hooker Chemical in Niagara County courts. Taken together, the suits were seeking up to $14 billion in damages. Residents also sought to sue the State of New York for failing to properly inspect building sites and warn residents of the potential health hazards of living in the area. Those claims totaled another $232 million.

The federal government also went to court to try to recover the enormous costs of cleaning up Love Canal and relocating its residents. In December 1979, the U.S. Justice Department sued Hooker Chemical for damaging the environment and forcing the government to declare a federal emergency. The department wanted Hooker to pay more than $117 million

in cleanup costs. It is the largest environmental suit the U.S. government had ever brought against a corporation. In 1980, the State of New York filed its own case against Hooker, seeking $635 million in damages.

The court cases dragged on for years as lawyers for the residents, attorneys for Hooker, attorneys for the state government, and attorneys for the federal government argued over who had the right to sue whom.

Eventually, the state and private suits were folded into the federal suits. But the first breakthrough didn't come until 1989 — more than a decade after

In 1979, U.S. Representative Al Gore from Tennessee began hearings on the crisis surrounding toxic dumping at Love Canal.

the crisis began. Occidental agreed to take over the costs of storing and destroying the waste from Love Canal. The agreement saved taxpayers more than $20 million in cleanup costs. More importantly, it was Occidental's first admission that it bore at least some responsibility for the disaster.

It wasn't until six years later, in December 1995, that Occidental finally agreed to pay $129 million in damages for Hooker's role in the dumping of toxic wastes at Love Canal. Coming seventeen years after the first lawsuits

"Good Neighbors"
"For Occidental, social responsibility is part of our core values. Social responsibility is about being the kind of progressive company that makes a difference in the communities where our employees live and work — particularly in developing countries. It is an integral part of managing our business well — as embodied in our 'Good Neighbor Policy.'"

— From the web site of Occidental Petroleum, which purchased Hooker Chemical

The Environmental Protection Agency monitors air, water, and soil quality. Workers wearing protective gear gather water samples for testing.

Love Canal was renamed Black Creek Village after the cleanup efforts. A local community agency successfully revitalized the area.

were filed, the victory brought little comfort to the families of Love Canal. Only $6.75 million of the money went to the victims themselves; a third of that amount was eaten up in attorney's fees. Affected families got awards ranging from $133,000 to as little as $63 for their years of suffering.

Action by Congress and the President

After Love Canal, voters were demanding that lawmakers act quickly to head off the dangers from toxic dumping. In 1979, a House subcommittee, chaired by a young Democratic representative from

Tennessee named Al Gore, began hearings on the crisis. Residents and officials from the State of New York and the EPA testified about growing health concerns. Representative Gore charged that Hooker could have prevented the disaster if it had heeded the warnings of its own employees that children were being burned by the toxic waters of the canal. Gore went on to make a name for himself in the environmental movement.

He later won election to the Senate, and in 1992 became vice president of the United States. The same year Gore became vice president, he published a best-selling book called *Earth in the Balance: Ecology and the Human Spirit*, which detailed the environmental problems facing the planet.

As the court cases surrounding Love Canal dragged into a second year, many lawmakers became convinced that the system for dealing with

Potential Health Effects of Chemical Compounds Identified at Love Canal

Compound	Acute Effects	Chronic Effects
benzaldehydes	allergen	
benzene	narcosis skin irritant	acute leukemia aplastic anemia pancytopenia chronic lymphatic leukemia lymphomas (probable)
benzoic acid	skin irritant	
carbon tetrachloride	narcosis hepatitis renal damage	liver tumors (possible)
chloroform	central nervous narcosis skin irritant respiratory irritant gastrointestinal symptoms	
dibromoethane	skin irritant	
dioxin	chloracne	nervous system disorders psychologic abnormalities cancer, spontaneous abortions, liver dysfunction (indicated in animal studies)
lindane	convulsions high white cell counts	
methylene chloride	anesthesia (increased carboxyhemoglobin)	respiratory distress death
trichloroethylene	central nervous depression skin irritant liver damage	paralysis of fingers respiratory and cardiac arrest visual defects deafness
toluene	narcosis (more powerful than benzene)	anemia (possible) leukopenia (possible)

Excerpted from A Special Report to the Governor and Legislature of New York State, April 1981.

CAUTION
HAZARDOUS WASTE SITE
DIOXIN CONTAMINATION
- **STAY IN YOUR CAR**
- **MINIMIZE TRAVEL**
- **KEEP WINDOWS CLOSED**
- **STAY ON PAVEMENT**
- **DRIVE SLOWLY**

USEPA, KANSAS CITY (816) 374-6529

Times Beach

Times Beach, Missouri — located just 25 miles (40 km) southwest of St. Louis — ranks among the most notorious of EPA Superfund sites. The oil the town had been spraying on roads to control dust was contaminated with dioxin. Contaminated soil washed into nearby creeks, contaminating the local water supply. By the time the EPA discovered the problem at Times Beach, dioxin contamination was so bad that the agency ordered the evacuation of the entire town. Tons of soil were excavated and burned to remove the dioxin contamination. Times Beach wasn't removed from the EPA Superfund priority list until 2001. It is now a Missouri State Park.

A large warning sign in Times Beach, Missouri, cautions motorists that they are passing into a toxic waste area contaminated by dioxin, a by-product formed in the production of many herbicides. A smaller sign to the left informs people of restricted access.

environmental disasters was seriously flawed. Toxic dumps required fast cleanup to protect the health of the people living around them. But how could these massive cleanups go forward if each one required the government to enter a multiyear lawsuit to recover the costs?

Congress responded by passing what became known as the Superfund Program in 1980. Administered by the EPA, Superfund is designed to find and clean up hazardous-waste sites around the country. The program includes the Superfund Trust Fund, which is a pool of money gained from special taxes on chemical and petroleum companies. When the companies responsible for contamination at a toxic-waste site cannot be found or lawsuits are pending, the money for the cleanup comes from the Superfund.

Superfund allowed the EPA to take what they call a "shovels first, lawyers later" approach to toxic-waste sites. The law meant that there would always be money for a cleanup, no matter how later court cases went. It also greatly expanded the EPA's role in regulating the nation's environment. Under the law, the EPA has investigated nearly 45,000 toxic-waste sites. More than 11,000 sites are constantly monitored, and it has helped with cleanup at more than 5,000 sites.

While many people were pleased that the government was taking a

> **"One of the Safest Places to Live"**
> "They must have cleaned it up pretty well. It's probably one of the safest places to live in Niagara Falls by now. There are problems no matter where you live in the world."
>
> — New Love Canal resident, interviewed in 1991

tougher approach to polluters, they were alarmed at how many of these sites existed. What was especially unnerving was that many of the toxic dumps were at U.S. military facilities, which have always been exempt from environmental regulations. Stunned voters found that their own government was one of the biggest toxic dumpers of all.

Return to Love Canal

In 1988, ten years after the Love Canal evacuations began, the New York State Department of Health announced that most areas of Love Canal were clean enough to live in again. Measured levels of toxicants had reached acceptable levels in all areas except those closest to the canal. New York State formed the Love Canal Area Revitalization Agency (LCARA) to sell abandoned homes in the area that had been refurbished.

Many former Love Canal residents were infuriated by the decision, feeling that no one could trust a government that had hidden the truth from them in the past. The reopening of the neighborhood brought angry protests. But slowly, people began to move into the area, attracted by home prices that were thousands of dollars lower than in surrounding neighborhoods.

In September 1999, after two decades of cleanup, the EPA announced that the cleanup work at Love Canal was finally finished. The agency proclaimed the area safe and said that two hundred wells throughout the neighborhood would monitor the area. By then LCARA had sold 239 homes in Love Canal, and plans were being made to invite business and industry back as well.

Love Canal is once again a quiet, middle-class community. Most of the homes that were abandoned by fearful residents are now sheltering families. The community even has a new name — Black Creek Village. Residents there feel safe in their new homes. Some point to the constant vigilance of state and federal monitors, a level of safety few other communities can boast. Some residents were just small children when the Love Canal crisis burst on the national scene and are only dimly aware of what the fuss was all about.

But no one in the environmental movement, no legislator or EPA administrator, no chemical manufacturer is likely to forget the name of Love Canal. In a strange way, the model city William T. Love imagined did become a part of history — not as a symbol of technology's bright promise, but as a reminder of the dangers that may lurk behind any new technology, no matter how innocent it may look on the surface.

Time Line

1893	William T. Love begins digging a canal on the Niagara River.
1920	Love's land is sold at auction to local power company.
1942	Hooker Chemical and Plastics Company begins to use Love Canal as a chemical waste dump.
1953	Hooker Chemical sells Love Canal to the Niagara Falls School District for $1.
1968	Hooker Chemical is purchased by Occidental Petroleum.
1975–76	Heavy rains and snow cause chemicals from Love Canal to surface.
1978	April: *Niagara Gazette* runs a series of articles on dumps in the Niagara area.
	April 25: New York State Commissioner of Health announces public health hazard at Love Canal.
1979	August 7: President Jimmy Carter declares Love Canal a federal emergency area.
	September: New York State evacuates two hundred more people from Love Canal.
	December: U.S. Department of Justice sues Hooker Chemical for $117 million.
1980	Congress passes the Superfund program.
1988	New York State Department of Health announces that most areas of Love Canal are safe to live in again.
1995	Occidental agrees to pay $129 million in damages.
1999	EPA announces that cleanup work at Love Canal is finished.

Glossary

alternating current (AC) a form of electricity in which electrons constantly change direction in a circuit; the kind of electricity that comes out of a wall outlet.

benzene (BEN zeen) a toxic chemical used in the production of plastics and fertilizers; it can cause cancer when inhaled or absorbed through the skin.

cancer an abnormal, uncontrolled increase in cell division that can spread through the body to overwhelm and invade healthy tissues.

carcinogen (kar SIN oh jehn) any substance that can cause cancer.

circa about; around; often used when referring to dates.

DDT (dichlorodiphenyltrichloroethane) a pesticide commonly used before 1970.

dioxins (dye AHKSS ihns) a group of highly toxic substances. Small levels of exposure to dioxins can cause cancer.

direct current (DC) a form of electricity in which electrons always move in one direction in a circuit; the kind of electricity provided by batteries.

DNA abbreviation for deoxyribonucleic acid, a complex molecule found in the nucleus of most cells that directs cell division and tissue differentiation.

EPA (Environmental Protection Agency) the federal agency in charge of setting and enforcing quality standards and guidelines for the protection of the environment. The EPA was established in 1970.

flamboyant a tendency away toward an elaborate approach in design, attitude, or action.

entrepreneur (on tra pre NYOUR) someone who owns and runs a business

leukemia (loo KEE mee uh) a blood cancer that affects the bone marrow and the production of white blood cells.

locks an area of a waterway with gates at each end that can raise or lower ships to different water levels.

miscarriage the death and/or loss of a fetus before birth.

mutagen (MYOO tuh jehn) any substance that causes mutations, or changes, in a cell's DNA.

mutation (myoo TAY shun) changes in DNA, sometimes caused by exposure to toxic chemicals; can cause deformed or abnormal growth.

PCB abbreviation for polychlorinated biphenyl; a type of industrial chemical that can cause cancer.

pollution the contamination of air, water, or soil with toxic substances.

Superfund the common name for the Comprehensive Environmental Response, Compensation, and Liability Act (CERCLA) — a federal program established in 1980 and run by the EPA that identifies and cleans up toxic-waste sites.

toxic a poison; also, the effects of a poison.

toxicant any poisonous substance, sometimes created by humans.

toxin a poison that has biological origins; can cause the production of antibodies in the blood of humans or animals and/or changes in that creature's DNA.

For More Information

Books

Chemical Accident. Christopher F. Lampton (Millbrook Press)

Love Canal. Great Disasters, Reforms, and Ramifications (series). Jennifer Bond Reed (Chelsea House)

Love Canal: Toxic Waste Tragedy. Victoria Sherrow (Enslow Publishers)

A River Ran Wild: An Environmental History. Lynne Cherry (Harcourt)

Techno-Matter: The Materials Behind the Marvels. Alfred B. Bortz (Twenty First Century Books)

Videos

Lois Gibbs and the Love Canal. (Trylon Video)

Industry and the Environment. (Congress Entertainment)

Volume 4: Pollution. Science in Action (series). (Vision Quest)

Stop That Dose! — Working Safely with Toxic Chemicals. (American Chemical Society)

Web Sites

Environmental Protection Agency — Superfund for Kids
www.epa.gov/superfund/kids/stories.htm

Love Canal Collection
ublib.buffalo.edu/libraries/projects/lovecanal/index.html

Superfund — Brief Success Stories for New York
www.epa.gov/superfund/programs/recycle/success/briefs/ny_brief.htm#ny_2

Superfund Stories
www.epa.gov/superfund/kids/stories.htm

Index